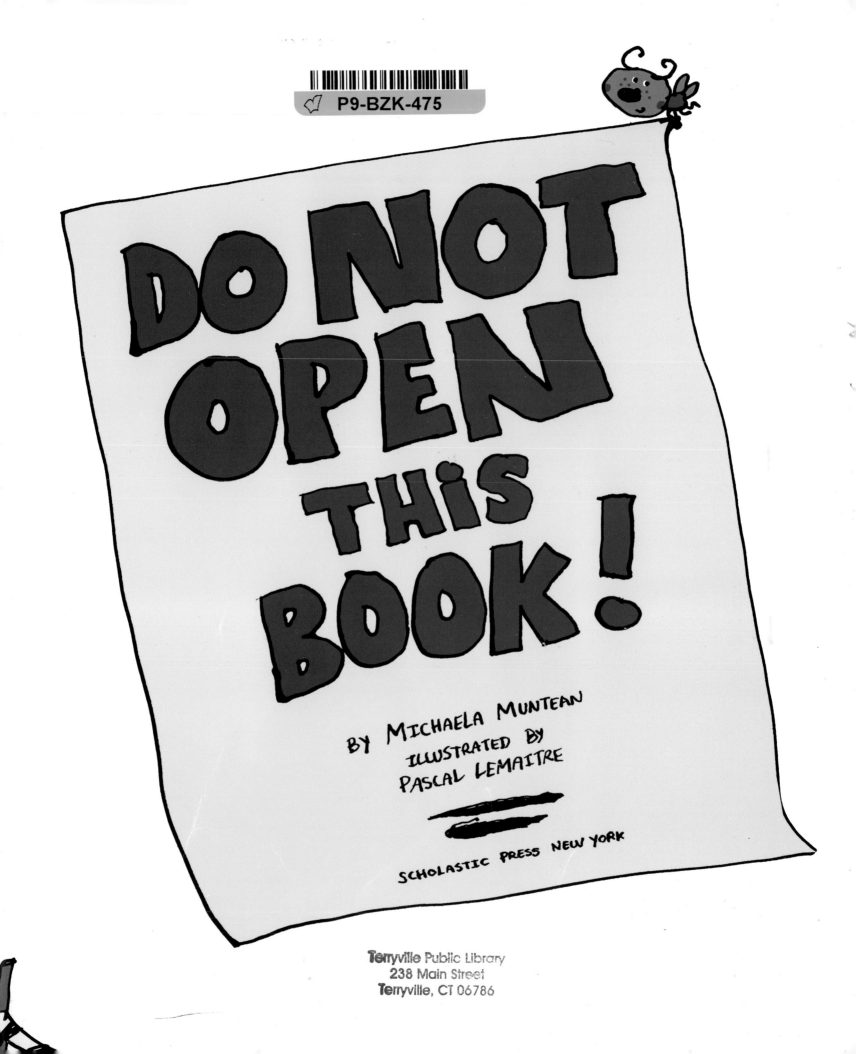

DO NOT OPEN THIS BOOK!

BY MICHAELA MUNTEAN

ILLUSTRATED BY PASCAL LEMAITRE

SCHOLASTIC PRESS NEW YORK

Library of Congress Cataloging-in-Publication Data

Muntean, Michaela. • Do not open this book / by Michaela Muntean; illustrated by Pascal Lemaitre.— 1st ed.   p. cm.

Summary: As Pig tries to write a book, he chastises the reader who keeps interrupting him by turning the pages.

ISBN 0-439-69839-1 (hardcover)

[1. Authorship—Fiction. 2. Books and reading—Fiction. 3. Pigs—Fiction.] I. Lemaitre, Pascal, ill. II. Title.

PZ7.M929Dn 2006   [E]—dc22   2005005580   10 9 8 7 6 5 4 3 2 1   06 07 08 09 10

Printed in Singapore 46   First edition, March 2006

All the text was hand-lettered by the artist.

The artwork was created using pen and ink, colored in Adobe Photoshop.

Book design by Pascal Lemaitre and Marijka Kostiw

For Maddie and Alex, who love words. —M.M.
To Linlin and Mahina from Maëlle Lemaitre. —P.L.

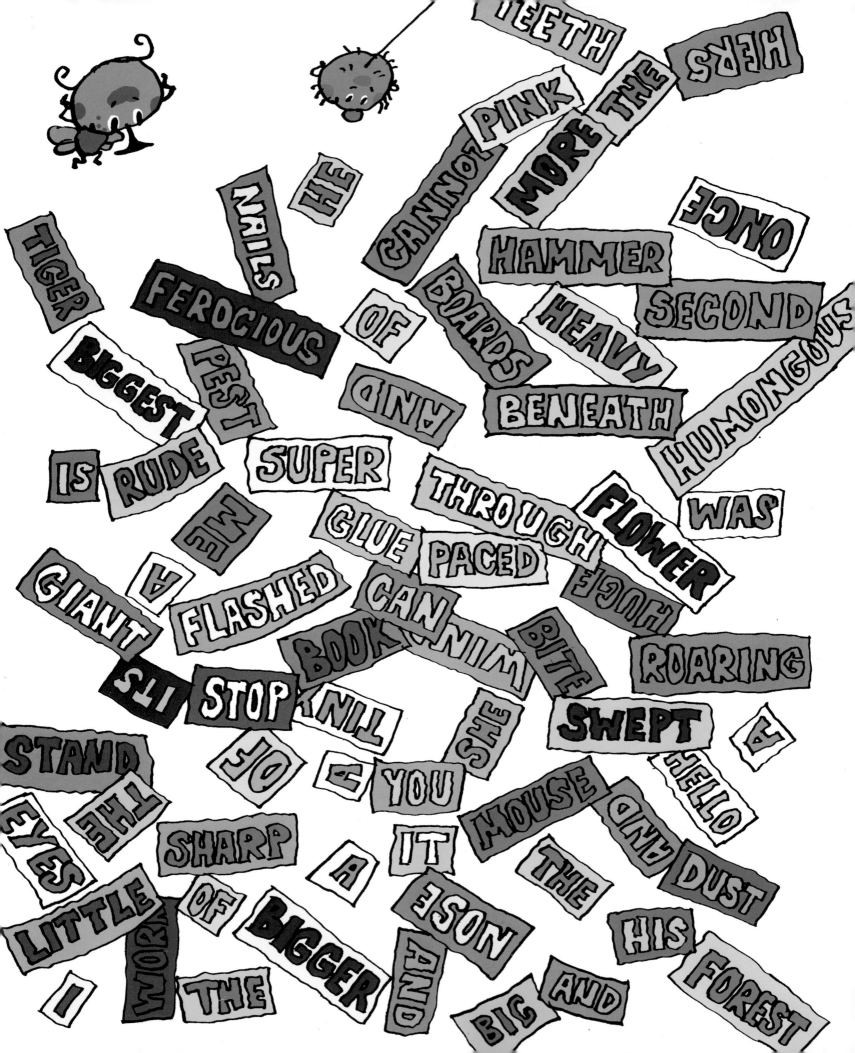

A FEROCIOUS STORM FOREST A TINY MOUSE FLOWER . A TIGER PACED SHARP TEETH TRYING THE ROARING

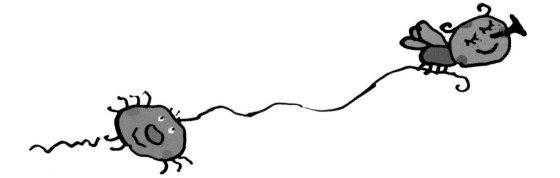

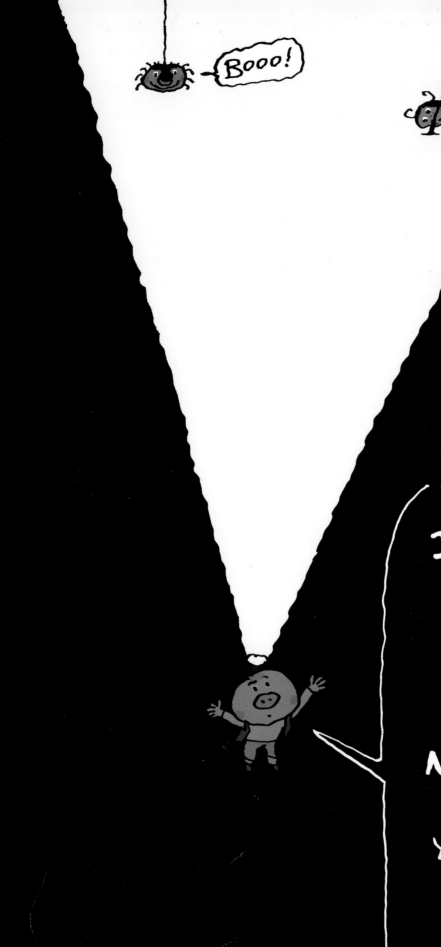

There once was a giant pest named

_____. _____ had huge eyes,

humongous ears, and too many teeth. Also,

a big nose. It did not matter how many

times _____ was asked to GO AWAY,

_____ would not go. Finally, I had to

call the Giant Pest Control Company.

"Hello," I said. "I am on page twenty-nine

of an unwritten book and a giant pest

named _____ will not stop bothering

me. I cannot work and I cannot stand

this for another second, so please send

someone right away to help me get rid

of _____."

IT WAS A BEDTIME STORY, TOO, BECAUSE I AM CERTAINLY VERY TIRED.

I AM GOING TO SLEEP NOW.

GOOD-BYE, AND...

OH... UM... THANK YOU FOR HELPING ME WRITE THIS BOOK.

I COULDN'T HAVE DONE IT WITHOUT YOU.

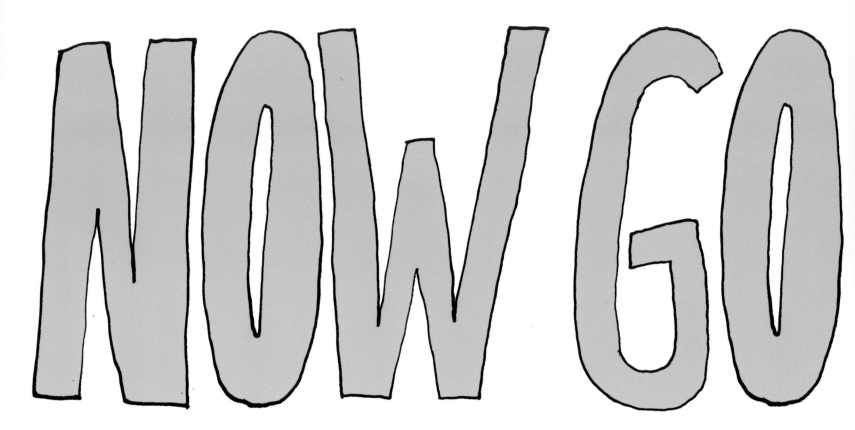